Cézanne

JOSEPH-ÉMILE MULLER

Cézanne

fernand hazan éditeur

35-37, RUE DE SEINE, PARIS-6ᵉ

TRANSLATION BY JANE BRENTON

© FERNAND HAZAN, PARIS, 1982
REPRODUCTION RIGHTS RESERVED

PRINTING 1987
BY PIZZI, MILAN
PRINTED IN ITALY

ISBN 2 85025 159 3

Impulse and order

There are painters who give expression in their work, directly or indirectly, to the things that move, uplift or torment them in life, and hence a detailed knowledge of their personal history is important to an understanding of the nature and development of their art. This is not true of Paul Cézanne. In his case biographical information is largely irrelevant and only rarely provides an insight into the paintings.

He was born in Aix-en-Provence on 19 January 1839. His father was a hat-maker who became a partner in a bank in 1848, a change in circumstances that undoubtedly benefitted the young Cézanne. Initially he had a private income and in 1886 inherited a considerable fortune. But whether he would have painted any differently, if he had been obliged to sell his paintings in order to live, is an entirely different question. On the whole it seems unlikely. All one can say with certainty is that his financial independence freed him from that particular pressure. Like most painters he was originally destined for a quite different career. After a classical education at the Collège Bourbon in Aix he bowed to his father's wishes and enrolled as a law student at the university. But the legal profession did not appeal to him, any more than a career in the offices of his father's bank, where he worked for a short while in 1861.

At school one of his fellow pupils and friends was Emile Zola, then writing poems and dreaming of a fortune as a writer. Cézanne too wrote poetry at that period of his life but, significantly, from 1856 onwards his main preoccupation was painting. Zola had moved to Paris in 1858, and in 1861 Cézanne followed suit, staying there for a few months and returning to the capital again at the end of 1862. Thereafter he was to divide his time between Paris and the South of France.

In Paris he worked at the Académie Suisse, an independent school of art also attended by Guillaumin and Pissarro. In 1862 he was introduced by them to Renoir, Sisley, Monet and Manet, and though not gregarious by nature attended some of their sessions at the Café Guerbois. In time the influence of these friends was to show itself in his painting, but at this stage he was still finding his way, looking above all to the example of the old masters in the Louvre (Italian, French and Spanish) and to the works of Delacroix, Daumier and Courbet. It should be said that his earliest pictures show one thing quite plainly – he was the very opposite of a youthful prodigy. Whatever the intensity of his feelings and beliefs, his ability to express them was only half-formed; his efforts are either tentative or uncontrolled.

The early paintings (1859–1862) are a fairly heterogeneous collection: *The Poet's Dream*, *The Four Seasons*, *Chinese Worshipping the Sun*, *Hide-and-Seek*, *The Visitation*, *Interior* – the titles alone indicate the range of subject matter. The style too varies from one extreme to the other, showing that Cézanne was still receptive to outside influences of the most diverse kind. In one picture he would use a chiaroscuro vaguely reminiscent of Caravaggio, in another he would copy Lancret or a fashion print from a magazine; in one instance he produced a work of such pronounced linear emphasis that he jokingly signed it 'Ingres, 1811'.

Inevitably his time in Paris taught him much about painting that he could never have learned in Aix. Still his subject matter remained varied: between 1863 and 1871, his pictures included a *Christ in Limbo*, an *Orgy*, a *Laying-Out*, a *Fisherman by the Riverside*, a *Murder* and a *Pastoral*. In addition there were portraits, landscapes and still-lifes. When he was dealing with imaginary scenes he became impassioned and sensual, often betraying a violence of temperament that readily gave way to baroque excess and melodrama; in his other works he tended to be more faithful to reality as he observed it. What the two strands of his painting have in common is a broad and free style, and on occassion a crude simplification of form. Sometimes he tried to copy the opulent colouring he admired in Véronèse, Rubens or Delacroix, sometimes his colour range was restricted and the effects were obtained essentially from the contrast of light and shade. The handling was rough and impulsive and he applied the pigment, often very thickly, with a palette knife. Usually the portraits were of members of his family (his father, sister Marie or uncle Dominique) or of his friends (Zola, Valabrègue, Boyer). Sometimes he painted self-portraits. Generally he represented no more than the sitter's face and a small part of the shoulders, and almost always the face was shown frontally or in three-quarters profile, with the eyes downcast. Rarely do the eyes seem to seek out our own. Even at this early stage Cézanne had little interest in setting up a dialogue with the onlooker.

When he painted someone sitting down, for example his father reading the newspaper *L'Evénement* or the Aix painter *Achille Emperaire* (a dwarf described by Joachim Gasquet as having 'a magnificent cavalier's head à la Van Dyck') he would show the body absolutely square on – but Emperaire's eyes are averted and his father's are directed firmly at his newspaper. And there is the same containment within the world of the picture in paintings such as *Zola Reading* and *Paul Alexis Reading a Manuscript to Zola*. The reader is totally absorbed in his text and Zola is concentrating on what he hears to the exclusion of all else.

The second of these two pictures remains of interest for other reasons: the rather squat figures are clearly defined by geometric shapes, contained within triangles that in turn are juxtaposed with vertical and horizontal lines. In terms of its composition it is one of the best orchestrated of Cézanne's youthful works.

When an artist is concerned to impose a pictorial discipline on the external world, the genre best suited to his purpose is likely to be the still-life. Cézanne quickly realised its many advantages, and indeed his still-lifes are easily his most accomplished paintings of the period around 1870. Two are particularly striking: *Still-life with Kettle* and *The Black Clock*. On the one hand the objects are realistically represented in terms of their characteristic appearance, and in that respect the paintings come close to Courbet; on the other hand each item has a purely pictorial function to fulfil. The smooth, regular and polished forms of the clock contrast with the baroque shape of the sea shell with its ridges, bumps and spines. Near the clock, the cloth folded back over the table flows into a number of convoluted folds; near the shell it assumes the stiff pleats and flat surfaces of starched material. The colour scheme too presents a satisfying tension between the light and dark shades.

The canvas is in another respect very typical of Cézanne: the objects are set fair and square in the foreground of the picture; it is as though they are placed right underneath our noses to insist that we register their presence. The composition has practically no depth at all.

In *Still-life with Kettle* the objects spread out on a shelf are less tightly grouped, though still carefully positioned. The cloth here is not stiff at all but is once again the pretext for a complex of curving lines. These provide a discreet sense of movement that is in keeping with the reposeful quality of the receptacles and the shelf on which they rest. Like *The Black Clock*, this canvas has the measured sobriety that is characteristic of many of Cézanne's later works.

Among the early landscapes are some reminiscent of Corot or Monticelli; others romantic or even Expressionist in mood, such as *L'Estaque under Snow* (1870); and yet others that give hints of the direction Cézanne was to take in the future. Of this last category none appears more significant than *Cutting with the Montagne Sainte-Victoire* (1870–1871). Not only because it is the first appearance in his work of the Montagne Sainte-Victoire, which was to play such a central role in his painting, but because the composition is so beautifully orchestrated, stressing the lines that give it shape and rhythm. The muted colours are akin to those of the still-lifes, and there is little sense of the pellucid brilliance of meridonal light or indeed of the open air at all.

Cézanne painted this picture at L'Estaque, where he

had gone to escape the Franco-Prussian War in 1870. No doubt he would have gone instead to Aix, but he wanted to conceal from his father that he was living with his model, Hortense Fiquet, who in 1872 bore him a son, Paul. Still fearful of his father's reaction he did not marry her until 1886.

Landscape with Tree. 1880-85.
Art Institute of Chicago

Links with Impressionism

When hostilities ceased Cézanne returned to Paris and soon afterwards went to live just outside the city (in Pontoise, Auvers-sur-Oise). There he worked alongside Pissarro, who was nine years his senior and was at the time producing the pictures that were to make him one of the central figures of the emergent Impressionist group. 'Even in 65,' Cézanne tells us, 'he had renounced black, bitumen, burnt Sienna and the ochres.' And as Pissarro recommended him to paint only with 'the three primary colours and their immediate derivatives', the younger painter decided to abandon what he called his 'fouled-up style' and to revise his palette entirely. He was however by no means an orthodox discipline of the movement that in 1874 came to be called Impressionist. Certainly he painted out of doors and from the motif, and he observed the effects of light and atmosphere, but he was not content merely to make his picture a record of the continual modification of coloured vibrations. Clinging to the solidity of forms – and the solidity of his own composition – he always laid stress on tangible, resistant objects such as walls, the roofs of houses, tree trunks and bare branches.

Although he did give a sense of depth to his panoramic landscapes he would usually employ some device to prevent the eye from straying into the far distance, often positioning a house where it would hold the attention, frequently at the end of a road or twisting path. He used this compositional feature in, for example, *Doctor Gachet's House at Auvers* (1873) –

Doctor Gachet being the art-loving medical practitioner who lived near him in Auvers and who was such an unfailing source of support for young experimental artists.

One of the most famous pictures of this period, *The House of the Hanged Man* (1873), shows a number of buildings hugging the contours of the ground. The one on the right is a compact mass pressed down by the ugly weight of its roof. Reinforcing the heavy solidity of the unwelcoming houses are other elements with attributes of hardness and aridity, notably the tall thin tree trunks bristling with bare branches. Even the light has none of the radiance so often seen in Impressionist works. The colour is harsh rather than harmonious. Here again Cézanne has used a heavy impasto, laboriously applying the paint in dabs. Explaining this technique he told Maurice Denis: 'It's because I can't express my feeling at the first attempt; so I put on more colour, I just go on putting it on. But at the outset I always mean to put on the whole of the pigment at once, like Manet, expressing the form with the brush.'

Shown to the public in 1874 at the first Impressionist Exhibition, *The House of the Hanged Man* was one of the works that aroused general mirth, although this did not prevent it being purchased by the Comte Doria. Another canvas exhibited by Cézanne on the same occasion attracted even more derision; this was *A Modern Olympia* (1873–1874). 'Alas!' wrote Louis Leroy in *Le Charivari*, 'Take a look at this one! A woman bent double, from whom a negress is removing the final veil to present her in all her ugliness to the fascinated inspection of a brown mannikin. You remember Monsieur Manet's *Olympia?* Well, that was a masterpiece of drawing, decorum and polish compared with that of Monsieur Cézanne.' For another reviewer Marc de Montifaud, who wrote for *L'Artiste*: '. . . this corner of an artificial paradise has taken away the breath of the boldest spirits . . . and Monsieur Cézanne seems like nothing so much as a kind of lunatic, racked, as he paints, with *delirium tremens*.'

Plainly Cézanne did have Manet in mind when he was working on this picture. But it is equally clear that his intention was to produce something quite different from Manet – and in that he certainly succeeded. The painting is (once again) very baroque in mood. Almost all the lines are convoluted and there is no hint of the flowing outline so dear to Manet. People and objects are reduced to little more than splashes of colour (pale or bright), energetically distributed. Unlike his predecessor, Cézanne emphasizes the third dimension of the room and also supplies a narrative framework, something entirely uncharacteristic of him in his later works.

The baroque elements that link this painting with the canvases of his first period are still to be seen in other compositions of the seventies, notably those depicting nudes, such as the *Bathers* or *The Battle of Love*.

Yet in the portraits of the same period there is nothing in the least overstated. In this they resemble his earlier portraiture, although the form and colouring are different. The models are always chosen from among Cézanne's family and friends, and his most frequent subjects were himself and his wife. It is not hard to guess why. For him portraits were paintings like any others and he wanted to be entirely free to concentrate on the achievement of his pictorial effects. Hence the need for docile and amenable models.

In his self-portraits Cézanne shows no inclination to unburden his soul or even to express how he is feeling at a particular time and place. To put it another way, he is not interested in painting his autobiography. But he does tell us something about his character; the man we see has a surly and suspicious side to his nature, he looks irritable and unsociable. Sometimes he seems a mixture of arrogance and insecurity, beset with doubts yet quickly roused to his own defence, for he was not unaware of his talents. In 1874 he wrote to his mother: 'I begin to feel I am better than those around me, and you know that the good opinion I have of myself is an entirely objective assessment.' In short, what the self-portraits reveal is a man who tends to prefer his own company and thoughts, more likely to rub people up the wrong way than to make friends.

When he uses his wife as his model the picture betrays not the least hint of affection. The face is normally impassive, expressionless, even bored, and could hardly be viewed with more detachment. Hortense Fiquet, for her part, must have sat for these portraits without any great interest or pleasure: she could hardly have failed to notice that in the final product her face would be reduced to a more or less perfect oval, without the slightest indication of her character or temperament. She is said to have been a talkative woman but here she gives the impression of being locked in a sullen silence from which she seems little disposed to emerge.

There is just one portrait from this period that appears to be more revealing of its subject's personality, and that is a picture of *Victor Chocquet*, a customs official who had a passion for the Impressionists' work, and for Renoir and Cézanne in particular. He was painted by both artists, and by Cézanne on a number of occasions. The first of these portraits (1876–1877) shows the head in three-quarters profile. With his noble brow framed by thick, unruly hair, and those thin elongated features seemingly consumed by some inner fire, Chocquet looks like one of the prophets or saints who appear in effigy over the doorways of Gothic cathedrals. Or he could be a modern counterpart of those characters of Byzantine art or in the works of El Greco, men transfigured by the intensity of their spiritual ardour. What comes as a shock is that the man we see in Renoir's portrait is another person entirely. The hair is not wiry and bushy, it is sleek and fine. The eyes are full of spirit but the face has a rather gentle expression, almost resigned, as though marked by traces of early hardship. So for Cézanne this ally of the Impressionists was an embattled and uncompromising disciple, for Renoir he was a kind but unimpassioned friend and supporter. The conclusion is inescapable: Cézanne, as ever, puts more of his own temperament into the portrait than that of his subject.

This painting was shown, with others, at the Impressionist Exhibition of 1877. And however admirable we may find it today, at the time it provoked renewed outbursts of derision and insults. But it did prompt Georges Rivière to write in *L'Impressioniste* that 'the artist who has been most attacked and ill-treated in the last fifteen years, by the press and public alike, is Monsieur Cézanne. There is no outrageous epithet that has not been attached to his name and the only success his works have achieved, and continue to achieve, is in making people hysterical with laughter.' He went on: 'These laughs and jibes are rooted in a bad faith that no one even troubles to hide. People go to see Monsieur Cézanne's pictures with the sole intention of having a good laugh. For my part I know of no painting less amusing than this ... Monsieur Cézanne is a painter, and a great painter at that.' Discerning and complimentary words, but the painter was upset by the general reaction to his work and decided to take no further part in the Impressionist exhibitions. A few months later he made up his mind to leave the Paris area and go to live in the South.

Smoker. 1890-92.
*Boymans Museum,
Rotterdam*

16

Beyond Impressionism

Cézanne did not entirely disappear from Paris and the Pontoise region; it was not in fact until 1882 that he made his principal home in Aix, and even then he returned occasionally to the banks of the Seine or visited some other part of France.

But as far as his painting was concerned, the break made him draw even further away from the Impressionists. He did not reject outright what he had learned from them; he retained the palette and the subject matter – or perhaps more accurately, he continued to favour the same subjects as they did, notably landscapes rather unremarkable in themselves. At the same time he wanted 'to make of Impressionism something solid and durable, like the art of the Museums and so he laid increasing emphasis on the framework of his pictures, stressing geometric elements and the contrasts between them. He also abandoned heavy impasto and applied his colour in hatching strokes, with the effect that it appears partially detached from the objects themselves. As he developed he saw the picture more and more as an autonomous organism. Certainly he was still concerned to express the sensations aroused in him by the external world, and indeed to express the sensations aroused in him by the external world, and indeed to express them with power and life, but he also wanted to impose an intellectual order on his painting. By no means an easy task, since the two aims are to some extent in conflict. Hence Cézanne's belief that 'an intelligence that is powerful at organisation is the most precious collaborator for the feelings in creating a work of art'. Hence too his constantly reiterated complaints, right up to his death, at the painfully slow progress of his work.

His feeling for the density of objects made trees a natural subject for him to paint, whether in the Paris region or in the South, poplars, chestnuts or orchards thick with undergrowth. I have referred already to his liking for tree trunks and bare branches. He did also paint foliage, though never with that flickering insubstantiality so dear to Monet. Nor was he even remotely interested in capturing the play of reflected light when he was dealing with an expanse of water or sea. For his treatment of seascapes one must look to a series of canvases painted between 1882 and 1886 at L'Estaque. It is immediately obvious that this is the Mediterranean: the water is calm and blue, luminous in the transparent air. But there is practically no suggestion of a wave to ruffle the surface. Still and flat, this sea stretches before us as though it is on the point of coagulating. It is framed by rocks or sweeps of land covered with trees, houses, factory chimneys, and these serve not only to enclose and counteract the fluidity, they also – through the interaction of the straight lines and curves that define them – provide a controlled animation that is in contrast with the peaceful surface of the water. Of course the clarity of the drawing derives at least in part from the dry and limpid southern air, just as the haze that envelopes the objects in the paintings of Monet, Pissarro and Sisley is an atmospheric effect recorded by these artists in the Ile-de-France. But there is the difference with Cézanne that he retained his sharply defined structures even when his subject was Lake Annecy or a bridge over the Marne.

While in the South he worked not only at L'Estaque but at Gardanne, in the Vallée de l'Arc and at the Jas de Bouffan, a house not far from Aix which his father had brought in 1859 and which he loved to visit.

What interested him particularly about Gardanne was the way the houses were arranged in tiers; his treatment of the buildings stresses their geometric form in a manner one mightr describe as pre-Cubist. Often the houses actually lean a little to the left. It would be an exaggeration to say you feel they are about to collapse, but certainly they hold the attention in a way they would not if perfectly upright. (Cézanne uses the same method of 'sensitising' our vision for trees, people and still-lifes.)

The Vallée de l'Arc posed a different kind of problem, that of suggesting a broad vista terminating in the profiled view of the Montagne Sainte-Victoire. Cézanne's solution is not to use the vanishing points of classical perspective. He does introduce a few oblique lines to encourage the eye to move over the plain into the background, but relies principally on alternating planes of ochre and green to represent the earth and the vegetation. The eye is encouraged to jump from one of these colours to the next, and so we enter into the space and move through it, exploring it freely yet without danger of becoming lost. Lines of varying lengths act as guides and there is a sense of re-assurance in experiencing such perfect order, so subtly disposed. The mountain itself is brought closer; Cézanne gives it the majestic presence and monu-mentality it has in his own mind.

The Montagne Sainte-Victoire was a motif he never seemed to tire of. In *c.* 1895–1900 he studied it from close to and emphasized the hardness and dominance of the rocky mass. Later he showed it in the distance, appearing to preside over the plain spreading out at its foot. In 1886 that plain was dotted with houses, trees and shrubs; fifteen or twenty years later all that remains are splashes of colour that have ceased to have a representational function and instead record the artist's subjective response to the scene before him. Yet there is nothing in the least formless or confused. By this date the mechanics of composition are well concealed but they are not neglected. In their style these late oils have come to resemble Cézanne's watercolours, already marvellously light and free in touch. Full of rapid and expressive abbreviations, they are proof of a quite staggering dexterity. That Cézanne achieved a similar fluency in his late oil-paintings is probably a direct result of his work on watercolours.

In 1904, again bemoaning the agonies of 'execution', he wrote: 'I think I get closer to it every day, although it's a rather laborious process. For, if a powerful feeling for nature – which I most certainly possess in abundance – is the necessary prerequisite for all artistic conception, the foundation on which rests the grandeur and the beauty of the finished work, no less essential is a knowledge of the methods of expressing our feelings, and that can be acquired only through long experience and practice.'

In other words, it was by sheer application and hard work that Cézanne achieved his mastery of technique. And perhaps that is why in the last ten years of his life he tended to choose difficult and, one might assume, unrewarding subjects – such as views of rocks, or the Bibémus Quarry. For the average person, what could be less appealing? But Cézanne found them exhilarating; again and again they inspired him to produce works of great beauty and feeling. Sometimes the eye is brought up against sheer cliffs, a maze of fissures and crags; sometimes the rocks form random patterns, like boulders hurled by angry clyclops; or blocks of stone lie scattered or in heaps near an abandoned mill-stone and a few thin tree trunks leaning at an angle. Nothing could be more lifeless or anonymous than these chunks of rock and stone. But Cézanne saw living things in the geological formations. For him they were a petrified history of the world. And, on another level, he relished their robust solidity as elements in his pictorial structure.

With many of the later landscapes one has the distinct impression that Cézanne deliberately set out to increase his problems. For instance, he dwells more on the foliage of trees than on their trunks – paying more attention to what is undefined and insubstantial than to what is solid and geometric by nature. In practice this meant that he had to work even harder to prevent the picture from succumbing to the decorative profusion of its subject matter. But his architectural spirit succeeds triumphantly; the paintings remain coherent and smoothly articulated, never fragmented or evanescent in the manner of so many Impressionist works. We should not forget that by the end of his life Cézanne was less concerned to represent objects as they were than to convey the force of his own reactions to them. As he wrote in 1905: '. . . the apprehensions of colour that make up light give rise to abstraction and therefore do not allow me to cover my canvas entirely, or to persist with the delimitation of objects when the points of contact are tenuous and delicate; hence the result that my image, or picture, is incomplete.' Incomplete it may be, in the sense of not being in all respects 'finished', but full of things to savour and enjoy.

Bathers. 1879-82.
Boymans Museum, Rotterdam

Painting as an end in itself

As we have seen, in 1869–1870 Cézanne discovered an affinity with the still-life, and it was a genre he continued to practise throughout his life. Apples, pears, oranges and onions, arranged in a fruit bowl or on a plate, or simply on a table; a cloth, a napkin, a length of stiffly pleated drapery; here and there a glass, a pitcher or a bottle – these were the elements with which he juggled. The table, only visible in part, might be set against a bare wall or a wallpapered surface, or it might be stood in front of a chest-of-drawers or (notably in 1895–1900) the ornate folds of a heavy, patterned curtain. Almost invariably the central feature was the fruit, though as Cézanne progressed he became less interested in its reality as flesh and substance. The forms and colours of the individual pieces of fruit, the way he placed them in groups or in isolation or balanced them precariously on top of each other, all these show that, fundamentally, he was interested in one thing only, the sheer eloquence with which they could be transposed into the picture. Cézanne's still-lifes are the clearest possible illustration of his belief that: '. . . drawing and colour are not separate things. To the extent that you paint you also draw. The more the colours harmonize, the more precise becomes the drawing. When the colour is at its richest, the form has reached plenitude. In the contrasts and relationships of the tones, there lies the secret of drawing and modelling.' Of course modelling in the usual sense does not exist in his work, and colour 'modulations' take the place of transitions from light passages to dark.

In a few of the still-lifes arrangements of flowers are included with the pears and apples, or on occasion form the principal motif of the composition. But flowers are by their nature insubstantial, and their complex and 'capricious' forms never held quite the same attraction for Cézanne as the firm, plump fruit. Since he spent a long time over each painting, the blossoms were very often faded before he had finished, and for that reason he often preferred artificial flowers. As a result his bouquets rarely have the spontaneous charm of flowers by Renoir or Manet, for example. In his *Blue Vase* (1885–1887) the blooms are, anyway, a less important feature of the composition than the large, stiff leaves and the various other items arranged nearby with a deceptively casual skill.

Whatever Cézanne's preference for still-lifes he also continued to paint portraits. Between 1880 and 1890 these were still usually restricted to a head-and-shoulders view of the sitter. There are again numerous self-portraits, in some of which the head is surmounted by a hat, its curves echoing those of the face. Otherwise the balding dome of the head appears as a convex mass, its solid geomatrical forms giving an immediate impression of the man's nature, his intensity and determination, not to say obstinacy. In one picture Cézanne (half-length) is standing before his easel, palette in hand. Very grave, his manner troubled but resolute, he looks directly towards us. The approximately rectangular surface of the palette contrasts with the curves formed by the shoulders and the head, and also with the sloping lines of the easel. 'Treat nature in terms of the cylinder, the sphere and the cone' – this was the principle he stated in 1904 to Emile Bernard.

And he applied it even to the human frame. After 1890 his models were usually shown seated, the body visible down as far as the knees. His portraits of his wife in this category are among his most remarkable. The forms are more geometrical, more precisely defined and more varied than in the earlier portraits, giving the sitter (whose individual character is still almost entirely neglected) a stark and impressive monumentality.

Also constructed on strict geometric principles are the portraits of the art critic *Gustave Geoffroy* (1895) and the dealer *Ambroise Vollard* (1899), who in 1895 organised the first major exhibition of Cézanne's work. Geffroy is wedged between his table and his book-shelves, and surrounded by books and note-books, making this one of Cézanne's most complex portraits. That of Vollard is considerably more straightforward in composition. The figure is seated, his legs crossed and his arms placed almost symmetrically in front of him; he has a characteristically somnolent air – something that must have appealed to Cézanne since he demanded long sessions of motionless posing from his sitters. It is said that after more than a hundred sittings he broke off from his work to say to Vollard 'I'm not displeased with the shirt-front' – that being only a tiny part of the picture.

There are four portraits painted in or around 1895 of the *Boy in a Red Waistcoat*. The most famous of these shows the boy sitting in a chair and turning to the right; he is supporting his head with his left arm, the elbow of which rests on the table. This arm, which is partially exposed, looks thin and stiff, almost wooden, while the other arm, concealed by the shirt-sleeve, is very long indeed and reaches right down to rest on the boy's knee. Anatomically it is incorrect, but viewed purely as an element of the picture it is superb. The German painter Max Liebermann put it very well when he said: 'The painting of this arm is so fine that I wish it were even longer.'

Cézanne also liked to paint peasants – hardly surprising as their reserve and taciturnity made them almost the perfect choice of subject for him. In most cases the figure appears alone, often resting his chin in his hand or smoking a pipe, always thoughtful and serious and rather withdrawn. When two or three appear together, playing a game of cards, there is some attempt to differentiate between them. Cézanne observes very well the attitudes adopted by the players and the concentration on their faces. But where another painter would have shown the men talking, shouting and gesticulating, Cézanne shows each one studying his cards, immobile, reflective, and paying scarcely any attention to his neighbour. Much of the picture's power comes from the tension between the players and the intensity of their absorption in a private world.

Yet the anecdotal qualities of these pictures are secondary. Once again it is the beauty of their composition that is paramount. The juxtaposition of triangles and rectangles, straight lines and curves, solids and hollows, is so sure and so eloquent that a kind of perfect harmony is created. Discipline and order are never merely schematic. Cézanne's feelings permeate each form, each patch of colour, and bring them an intense emotional conviction.

In the nude paintings too there is the same strength of feeling, the same rigorous construction. For a long time his nudes were sensual and baroque, but during the eighties the sensuality began to abate; the flesh became less rounded, less heavy, less palpable. Perhaps there is an underlying process of sublimation, certainly a progressive movement towards abstraction. The evolution is more rapid in the *Male Bathers* than in the *Female Bathers*. A picture of male nudes of *c.* 1890 reminds one of a late El Greco, so elongated and de-materialised are the bodies – effectively no more than malleable elements forming part of a rhythmic ensemble. For the female nudes the same trend reaches a triumphant culmination in *The Large Bathers* (1898–1905). To a realist nothing could appear more arbitrary than this group of nudes, nothing could make less narrative sense than this assembly of bodies, standing, crouching or reclining, whose sole purpose for existing is to form a decorative garland, teeming with life – but a life that does not relate to anything outside the context of the picture. There is no attempt to exploit sexual attraction or physical charms, in fact most of the bodies are unnaturally tall and lean. The poses they adopt make no sense at all, unless you view them as the artist intended, as complexes of lines and shapes. The same holds true for the landscape. The tree trunks slope towards each other simply so that they will form a triangle to enclose the two pyramids made by the bathers. The clouds are massed together in such a way as to echo the women's silhouettes. The picture is put together like a poem – it has rhyme and rhythm, correspondences and contrasts. One understands what Cézanne meant when he said he wanted to 're-do Poussin from nature'. Of course it was not his intention to copy his predecessor, but to re-interpret the principles according to which he painted. Cézanne's style remains entirely personal, and is inevitably more abstract than that of a seventeenth century artist.

Landscape. 1880-85.
Art Institute of Chicago

The influential theorist

In a letter to Emile Bernard of September 1906 Cézanne wrote: 'I have sworn to die painting.' It was a few weeks after that, when painting on the road to Tholonet, that Cézanne was drenched by a sudden downpour and collapsed. Not long afterwards, on 22 October, he died of pneumonia.

'I work in my own stubborn way,' he wrote in 1903 to Ambroise Vollard, 'and I can glimpse the Promised Land. Will I be like the great Hebrew leader or will I be able to enter it?' He went on: 'I've made some progress. But why so late and so laboriously? Is Art in truth a ministry that demands everything of its devotees?' Extraordinary to think that such ideas should come from a man so blessed with creativity and vision. Indeed his humility about his work did not inhibit him from a strong sense of his own worth. We have mentioned the terms in which he wrote to his mother in 1874. And at a later date Vollard claims he heard him say: 'You know very well there is only one painter in the world, and that is me.' When Zola in his novel *L'Oeuvre* of 1885–1886 created the character of a painter who was overcome with frustration 'because he could not make his genius bear fruit and killed himself before his unfinished work', Cézanne felt this was a direct attack on him and quarrelled irrevocably with the friend he had known since childhood. 'I am a trailblazer,' he wrote, 'others will follow.' And: 'I remain the originator of the path that I discovered.' He was of course perfectly correct, many of the concerns of modern painting arise directly out of his work. 'In the

Farm Gate in Auvers-sur-Oise. Etching.
Bibliothèque Nationale, Paris

beginning was Cézanne', the Cubist painter André Lhote was to declare, describing him also as 'one of our most precious theorists'.

Cézanne's influence in fact became apparent well before the Cubist era. It is to be seen in the work of Gauguin and also the young painters of the nineties who called themselves the Nabis; there is a well-known picture by Maurice Denis called *Homage to Cézanne* (1900), which shows a Cézanne still-life (recently acquired by Gauguin) surrounded by the figures of Redon, Bonnard, Vuillard, Ranson, Roussel etc. At around the same time Matisse became the owner of the *Three Bathers* (1879–1882), a picture that he studied closely and had particularly in mind when he painted *Luxury* (1907). As late as 1904 it was possible for Camille Mauclair to write: 'The name of Cézanne will continue to be associated with the most memorable artistic leg-pull of the last fifteen years.' But the artists and the innovators of the age worshipped his name and regarded him as an ideal to strive for. Even the ebullient Vlaminck went through his Cézanne period, and the same is true of other Expressionists. As for the Cubists, Braque or Picasso, Delaunay or Léger, Lhote or La Fresnaye, each one acknowledged the debt he owed to the Aix painter. More recently, it was above all Cézanne who inspired the movement of resurgent modernism in France at the time of the last war. One of these painters, Estève even painted his own *Homage to Cézanne* (1942) to express his fervent admiration for his predecessor.

But of course a painter's importance is not to be judged chiefly by the influence he exercised on others. It depends principally on the response to the work itself, independent of its historical context. And on that point there can be little argument that Cézanne has given us a body of work almost unsurpassed in its ability to move and delight the lover of painting. I have made frequent reference to the role construction plays in his work, to the eloquence he gave to his forms and the ways in which they are linked and balanced. But one should not underestimate either the expressive power and lyricism of his colour. His palette is not particularly brilliant; the pictures are not vibrant but they are immensely and satisfyingly alive. In the mature works each tint quivers, each dab of paint throbs with feeling, and all the harmonies are perfect. Not because they are an exact copy of nature but because, in metamorphosing the natural world, the painter is as unerring in the combinations of his invented colours as he is in the combinations of the forms they inhabit. Trying to arrive at a definition of classicism (in the broad sense), Henri Focillon noted 'that it is the point of the highest compatibility of the parts between themselves'. If we accept that definition we may conclude that Cézanne, after his exuberant beginnings and in spite of a certain tendency to over-statement that declared itself on occasion even late in his career, was essentially a classical painter, using that term in its finest and most complimentary sense.

Portrait of Cézanne, 1904
Bibliothèque Nationale, Cabinet des Estampes, Paris

On the cover:
L'Estaque Seen from the Gulf
of Marseille, detail, 1878-1879

List of plates

16 *The Sea at l'Estaque,* 1883-1886, oil. Picasso Donation.

17 *L'Estaque, Seen from the Gulf of Marseille,* circa 1878-1879, oil on canvas, 59,5 × 73 cm. Paris, Musée d'Orsay.

18 *View of l'Estaque and the Château d'If,* 1883-1885, oil, 71 × 57,7 cm. Cambridge, Fitzwilliam Museum.

19 *House in Bellevue,* circa 1883, oil. Geneva, private collection.

20 *The Bay of Marseille, Seen from l'Estaque,* 1884-1886, oil, 73 × 100 cm. New York, Metropolitan Museum of Art.

21 *Trees and Houses,* 1885-1887, oil on canvas, 54 × 73 cm. Paris, Musée de l'Orangerie, Walter Guillaume Collection.

22 *View of Gardanne,* 1885-1886, watercolor. New York, Brooklyn Museum.

23 *Flowers and Fruit,* circa 1886, oil on canvas, 35 × 21 cm. Paris, Musée de l'Orangerie, Walter Guillaume Collection.

24 *Vase of Tulips with Apples,* 1890-1894, oil on paper with cardboard backing, 72,5 × 42 cm. Chicago, Art Institute.

25 *Sainte-Victoire Mountain, Seen from Bellevue,* 1882-1885, oil, 65,5 × 81,7 cm. New York, Metropolitan Museum of Art.

26 *Sainte-Victoire Mountain, Seen from Around Gardanne,* 1886-1890, oil, 62,5 × 91 cm. Washington, National Gallery of Art.

27 *Sainte-Victoire Mountain, Seen from Bibémus,* circa 1887, oil, 65 × 81 cm. Baltimore Museum of Art, Cone Collection.

28 *The Red Rock,* circa 1895, oil, 92 × 68 cm. Paris, Musée de l'Orangerie, Walter Guillaume Collection.

29 *Sainte-Victoire Mountain,* 1889-1890, watercolor and graphite, 30,9 × 46,7 cm. Cambridge, Fogg Art Museum, Harvard University.

30 *Sainte-Victoire Mountain, See from Les Lauves,* 1904-1905, watercolor. Basel, Galerie Beyeler.

31 *Flowers and Fruit,* 1890-1894, oil. London, Courtauld Institute Galleries.

32 *Basket of Apples,* 1890-1894, oil. Chicago, Art Institute.

33 *Peasant in a Blue Smock,* 1895-1897, oil, 80 × 63,5 cm. Private collection, U.S.A.

34 *Woman with Coffeepot,* 1890-1895, oil, 130 × 96,5 cm. Paris, Musée d'Orsay.

35 *The Card Players,* 1890-1895, oil, 47,5 × 57 cm. Paris, Musée d'Orsay.

36 *Smoker or Man with Pipe,* circa 1890-1895, oil, 91 × 73 cm. Moscow, Pushkin Museum.

37 *Madame Cézanne in the Greenhouse,* circa 1890, oil, 92 × 73 cm. New York, Metropolitan Museum of Art.

38 *The Curtains,* 1885-1890, watercolor over graphite sketch, 49,1 × 30,5 cm. Paris, The Louvre, Cabinet des dessins.

39 *Pot of Geraniums with Fruit,* 1890-1894, oil. New York, Metropolitan Museum of Art.

40 *Still Life with Plaster Cast of Cupid,* circa 1895, oil on paper with cardboard backing, 70 × 57 cm. London, Courtauld Institute of Art.

41 *Young Man in Red Waistcoat,* 1894-1895, oil, 80 × 64,5 cm. Zurich, E.G. Bührle Collection.

42 *Portrait of Gustave Geffroy,* 1895, oil. Paris, Musée d'Orsay.

43 *Still Life with Onions,* 1895, oil, 66 × 82 cm. Paris, Musée d'Orsay.

44 *Small Boat and Bathers,* circa 1890, oil, 30 × 125 cm. Paris, Musée de l'Orangerie, Walter Guillaume Collection. (This is the middle section of a panel which was painted for Victor Chocquet around 1890 and later cut up into three parts. When the side sections came into the French State's possession with the Walter Guillaume Collection, it became possible to reconstitute the original work.)

45 *Five Women Bathing,* 1879-1882, oil. Picasso Donation.

46 *Bathers,* 1890-1892, oil, 60 × 82 cm. Paris, Musée d'Orsay.

47 *Women Bathing,* 1894-1905, oil, 136 × 191 cm. London, National Gallery.

48 *Group of Seven Bathers,* circa 1900. Basel, Galerie Beyeler.

49 *Foliage,* 1895-1900, watercolor and graphite, 44,8 × 56,8 cm. New York, Museum of Modern Art.

50 *Still Life with Pomegranate,* 1902-1906, watercolor and graphite, 31,5 × 47,6 cm. Basel, Galerie Beyeler.

51 *Still Life: Apples, Pears, and a Pan,* 1900-1904, graphite and watercolor on white paper, 28,1 × 47,8 cm. Paris, The Louvre, Cabinet des dessins.

52 *Still Life with Carafe,* circa 1900-1906, watercolor, 30 × 40 cm. Paris, Musée d'Orsay.

53 *Still Life: Apples, a Bottle, and the Back of a Chair,* 1902-1906, watercolor over graphite, 44,5 × 59 cm. London, Courtauld Institute Galleries.

54 *Garden Terrace in Les Lauves,* 1902-1906, graphite and watercolor. New York, private collection.

55 *Sainte-Victoire Mountain,* 1904-1906, oil, 63,5 × 83 cm. Zurich, Kunsthaus.

56 *Rocks near the Caves above the Château Noir,* circa 1904, oil, 65 × 54 cm. Paris, Musée d'Orsay.

57 *Château Noir,* 1904-1906, oil. Picasso Donation.

58 *Fishing,* 1904-1906, watercolor and graphite, 12,5 × 22 cm. Tokyo, The National Museum of Western Art.

59 *Portrait of the Artist Wearing a Beret,* 1898-1900, oil, 63,3 × 50,8 cm. Boston, Museum of Fine Arts.

PLATES

1
Nature morte à la bouilloire
1869
Still Life with Kettle

2
Nature morte
à la pendule de marbre noir
1869-1871
Still Life
with Black Marble Clock

3
Carrefour de la rue Saint-Rémy
vers 1873
Rue Saint-Rémy Intersection

4
La Maison du pendu
1873
The House of the Hanged Man

5
La Maison du docteur Gachet à Auvers, vers 1873
Doctor Gachet's House in Auvers

7
Le Déjeuner sur l'herbe
1873-1875
Luncheon on the Grass

8
Une moderne Olympia
1873-1875
A Modern Olympia

9
L'Après-midi à Naples
(avec servante noire)
1876-1877
A Naples Afternoon
(with Black Maid)

10
Paysage au toit rouge
(le pin à l'Estaque)
1876
Landscape with Red Roof
(Pine Tree at l'Estaque)

11
L'Estaque, effet du soir
L'Estaque in the Evening

12
Le Pont de Maincy
vers 1879
Maincy Bridge

13
Les Peupliers
1879-1880
Poplar Trees

14
Autoportrait
1879-1882
Self-Portrait

15
Madame Cézanne
au jardin
1880-1882
Madame Cézanne
in the Garden

16
La Mer à L'Estaque
1883-1886
The Sea at L'Estaque

17
L'Estaque
vue du golfe de Marseille
1878-1879
L'Estaque
Seen from the Gulf of Marseille

18
Vue sur l'Estaque
et le château d'If
1883-1885
View of l'Estaque
and the Château d'If

19
La Maison de Bellevue
vers 1883
House in Bellevue

20
La Baie de Marseille
vue de l'Estaque
1884-1886
The Bay of Marseille,
Seen from l'Estaque

21
Arbres et maisons
1885-1887
Trees and Houses

23
Fleurs et fruits
vers 1886
Flowers and Fruit

24
Vase de tulipes
et pommes
1890-1894
Vase of Tulips
with Apples

25
La Montagne Sainte-Victoire
vue de Bellevue
1882-1885
Sainte-Victoire Mountain
Seen from Bellevue

26
La Montagne Sainte-Victoire
vue des environs de Gardanne
1886-1890
Sainte-Victoire Mountain
Seen from Around Gardanne

27
La Montagne Sainte-Victoire
vue de Bibémus
vers 1887
Sainte-Victoire Mountain
seen from Bibémus

29
Montagne Sainte-Victoire
1889-1890
Sainte-Victoire Mountain

30
La Montagne Sainte-Victoire
vue des Lauves
1904-1905
Sainte-Victoire Mountain
Seen from Les Lauves

31
Fleurs et fruits
1890-1894
Flowers and Fruit

32
La Corbeille de pommes
1890-1894
Basket of Apples

33
Paysan en blouse bleue
1895-1897
Peasant in a Blue Smock

34
Femme à la cafetière
1890-1895
Woman with Coffee pot

36
Fumeur
ou l'Homme à la pipe
1890-1895
Smocker
or Man with Pipe

35
Les Joueurs de cartes
1890-1895
The Card Players

37
Madame Cézanne
dans la serre
vers 1890
Madame Cézanne
in the Greenhouse

38
Les Rideaux
1885-1890
The Curtains

39
Pot de géraniums et fruits
1890-1894
Pot of Geraniums with Fruit

40
Nature morte
avec l'Amour en plâtre
vers 1895
Still Life
with Plaster Cast of Cupid

41
Le Jeune Homme au gilet rouge
1894-1895
Young Man in Red Waistcoat

43
Nature morte aux oignons
1895
Still Life with Onions

44
La Barque et les Baigneurs
vers 1890
Small Boat and Bathers

45
Cinq Baigneuses
1879-1882
Five Women Bathing

47
Les Grandes Baigneuses
1894-1905
Women Bathing

48
Groupe de sept baigneurs
vers 1900
Group of Seven Bathers

49
Feuillage
1895-1900
Foliage

50
Nature morte à la grenade
1902-1906
Still Life with Pomegranate

51
Nature morte
pommes, poires
et casserole
1900-1904
Still Life
Apples, Pears
and a Pan

52
Nature morte à la carafe
1900-1906
Still Life with Carafe

53
Nature morte
pommes, bouteille et dossier de chaise
1902-1906
Still Life
Apples, a Bottle, and the Back of a Chair

54
La Terrasse du jardin des Lauves
1902-1906
Garden Terrace in Les Lauves

55
La Montagne Sainte-Victoire
1904-1906
Sainte-Victoire Mountain

56
Rochers près des grottes
au-dessus du Château Noir
vers 1904
Rocks near the Caves
above the Château Noir

57
Le Château Noir
1904-1906
Château Noir

58
La Pêche
1904-1906
Fishing

59 Portrait de l'artiste au béret, 1898-1900. Portrait of the Artist Wearing a Beret

COLLECTION LES MAÎTRES DE L'ART
MASTERS OF ART COLLECTION

* disponible en anglais
  available in english